MICHAEL'S RACING MACHINE

I Wonder Why

MICHAEL'S RACING MACHINE

By **Lawrence F. Lowery**

Illustrated by Richard Loehle

NSTA **Kids**
National Science Teachers Association

Claire Reinburg, Director
Wendy Rubin, Managing Editor
Andrew Cooke, Senior Editor
Amanda O'Brien, Associate Editor
Amy America, Book Acquisitions Coordinator

ART AND DESIGN
Will Thomas Jr., Director
Joseph Butera, Cover, Interior Design
Original illustrations by Richard Loehle

PRINTING AND PRODUCTION
Catherine Lorrain, Director

NATIONAL SCIENCE TEACHERS ASSOCIATION
David L. Evans, Executive Director
David Beacom, Publisher

1840 Wilson Blvd., Arlington, VA 22201
www.nsta.org/store
For customer service inquiries, please call 800-277-5300.

Lexile® measure: 680L

NSTA is committed to publishing material that promotes the best in inquiry-based science education. However, conditions of actual use may vary, and the safety procedures and practices described in this book are intended to serve only as a guide. Additional precautionary measures may be required. NSTA and the authors do not warrant or represent that the procedures and practices in this book meet any safety code or standard of federal, state, or local regulations. NSTA and the authors disclaim any liability for personal injury or damage to property arising out of or relating to the use of this book, including any of the recommendations, instructions, or materials contained therein.

Library of Congress Cataloging-in-Publication Data

Lowery, Lawrence F., author.
  Michael's racing machine / Lawrence F. Lowery ; illustrated by Richard Loehle.
      pages cm -- (I wonder why)
  Audience: K to 3.
  ISBN 978-1-941316-05-4 -- ISBN 978-1-941316-97-9 (e-book)
  1. Machinery--Juvenile literature. 2. Power (Mechanics)--Juvenile literature. I. Loehle, Richard, illustrator. II. Title.
  TJ147.L73 2014
  629.22'9--dc23
                            2014019375

Cataloging-in-Publication Data are also available from the Library of Congress for the e-book.

Safety note for teachers, parents, and students: When using tools such as those in this story, always maintain a safe environment. Most notably, wear personal protection including safety goggles and gloves as appropriate and take recommended safety precautions at all times.

Introduction

The *I Wonder Why* series is a set of science books created specifically for young learners who are in their first years of school. The content for each book was chosen to be appropriate for youngsters who are beginning to construct knowledge of the world around them. These youngsters ask questions. They want to know about things. They are more curious than they will be when they are a decade older. Research shows that science is students' favorite subject when they enter school for the first time.

Science is both *what* we know and *how* we come to know it. What we know is the content knowledge that accumulates over time as scientists continue to explore the universe in which we live. How we come to know science is the set of thinking and reasoning processes we use to get answers to the questions and inquiries in which we are engaged.

Scientists learn by observing, comparing, and organizing the objects and ideas they are investigating. Children learn the same way. The thinking processes are among several inquiry behaviors that enable us to find out about our world and how it works. Observing, comparing, and organizing are fundamental to the more advanced thinking processes of relating, experimenting, and inferring.

The five books in this set of the *I Wonder Why* series focus on some content of the physical sciences. The physical sciences consist of studies of the physical properties and interactions of energy and inanimate objects as opposed to the study of the characteristics of living things.

Physics, along with mathematics and chemistry, is one of the fundamental sciences because the other sciences, such as botany and zoology, deal with systems that seem to obey the laws of physics. The physical laws of matter, energy, and the fundamental forces of nature govern the interactions between particles and physical entities such as subatomic particles and planets.

These books introduce the reader to several basic physical science ideas: exploration of the properties of some objects (*Rubber vs. Glass*), interaction with the properties of light and the effect of light on objects (*Light and Color; Dark as a Shadow*), the nature of waves and sound (*Sounds Are High, Sounds Are Low*), and the use of simple machines to accomplish work (*Michael's Racing Machine*).

The information in these books leads the characters and the reader to discover how opaque objects block light and cast shadows, that different objects have special and useful properties (glass and rubber), that simple mechanical tools reveal some of the laws of physics, and that "nontouchable items" such as light and sound energy also have distinctive properties.

Each book uses a different approach to take the reader through simple scientific information. One book is expository, providing factual information. Several are narratives that allow a story involving properties of objects and laws of physics to unfold. Another uses poetry to engage the characters in hands-on experiences. The combination of different styles of artwork, different literary ways to present information, and directly observable scientific phenomena brings the content to the reader through several instructional avenues.

In addition, the content in these books supports the criteria set forth by the *Common Core State Standards*. Unlike didactic presentations of knowledge, the content is woven into each book so that its presence is subtle but powerful.

The science activities in the Parent/Teacher Handbook section in each book enable learners to carry out their own investigations related to the content of the book. The materials needed for these activities are easily obtained, and the activities have been tested with youngsters to be sure they are age appropriate.

After completing a science activity, rereading or referring back to the book and talking about connections with the activity can be a deepening experience that stabilizes the learning as a long-term memory.

One Saturday morning Michael decided to build a soapbox racing car. He had been thinking about building one for a long time. He found a set of plans in a magazine. The plans showed how to build a racing car.

Michael was studying the plans when Luci, the girl next door, saw him through the window.

Luci was two years younger than Michael. She was curious and always wanted to learn new things.

She rushed downstairs to find out what Michael was doing.

"Michael," asked Luci, "are you going to build something?"

Michael was so busy reading his plans, he did not hear Luci's question.
"What are you going to make?" Luci asked again.

"A racing car," said Michael. "I'm going to build the fastest racing car in the world. Dad is letting me use some of his tools to build it."

Michael began sorting the tools his father let him use.

"I know how hammers and saws work," said Luci, "but I don't know about some of the other tools."

"Well," said Michael, "all these tools help you do work. They are like machines." He pointed to some. "Screwdrivers, pliers. Even the broom in this room can be a helpful machine."

"I thought machines were great big things," Luci said, "like dishwashers and automobiles and lawnmowers." Her eyes were wide open now that Michael was showing her the tools.

Michael looked up at Luci and said, "Yes, those are machines. But a machine can be as tiny as a toothpick or as big as a trailer truck—even bigger. Have you ever seen a giant crane? Some are bigger than a house and are made of hundreds of smaller machines."

Michael picked up a crowbar and used it to lift a nail out of an old board.

"Is that thing a machine?" Luci asked.

"Yes. It's a crowbar. It makes my work easier. I couldn't pull the nail out by myself. With this machine's help, I can. It pulls the nail out when I push it here. Watch." Michael pulled a nail out.

Michael handed the crow bar to Luci and let her use it to pull out another nail.

"A machine like this is called a lever," Michael explained. "Any stiff bar that works this way is called a lever. Levers are all over the place."

"Where?" asked Luci. "I don't see any levers except the one you showed me how to use."

"Here!" Michael demonstrated. "This hammer is a lever. It's stiff like a crow bar and it lifts where the nail goes into the wood."

"Look," Michael went on, "you can take the next nail out yourself."

Luci took the hammer and used it to pull a nail out of a piece of wood.

"Doesn't that make pulling out a nail easier?" Michael continued. "Sticks and poles and bars and rods can all be used as levers."

"Do you mean that anything with a shape like a stick or a pole can be a machine?" Luci asked.

"Uh-huh. Look!" Just then Michael took a broom from the closet and swept the floor to show how the broom worked like a lever.

When he finished sweeping, Michael used the broom to hold the door open. Luci began asking more questions.

"Are there any other machines besides levers?"

"Lots," said Michael.

"Name one," insisted Luci.

"A wedge. A wedge is another machine," Michael replied. "A wedge is like a hill. A wedge is a simple machine because a hill is a simple machine."

"How can a hill be a machine?" asked Luci. "I don't understand that at all."

"Well," began Michael, "suppose you wanted to lift something up to a higher place but it was too heavy to lift. You might be able to raise the thing by pushing or pulling it up a hill. Moving something up a hill makes the work seem easier to do. That is why when you use a hill, it is a machine."

"Any hill is a machine," said Michael, "even a real hill that makes it easier for you to climb up a mountain."

Michael remembered that he was amazed when he learned that, at times, a real hill was a machine. He said, "I think that anything that even looks like a hill can be a machine."

"Do you mean like a flight of stairs?" wondered Luci.

"Right," said Michael.

Michael began sawing the first piece of wood for the racing car.

"A saw—is that a machine, too?" Luci asked.

"Sure," Michael responded, "the little teeth are like tiny hills that push the wood apart. Here, Luci. Do you see the tiny hills?"

Luci looked closely and did see the hills.

"These little hills are called wedges," said Michael.
"They are like two hills side by side that push things apart.
I think Abraham Lincoln must have used wedges to split logs."

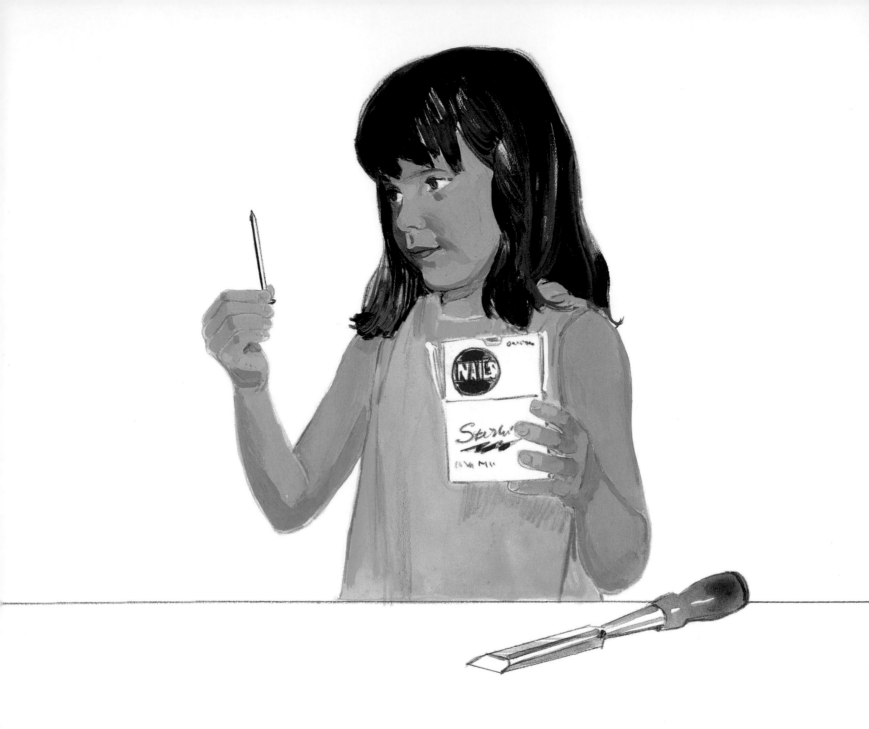

"Let's look for more wedges," said Luci.
She began looking at Michael's collection of tools.

"Here are some wedges," said Luci, smiling as she
found a box of nails. "The tiny points are like tiny hills."

Michael showed Luci a box of screws. Each screw looked like it had a tiny hill wrapped around a tiny pole.

"Look," said Michael, "if you think about it, you can imagine a road winding around a mountain. That makes a screw a machine, too, because it is like a winding hill, and remember, a hill can make work easier to do."

Michael finished cutting the wood and began
nailing the first pieces of the racing car together.
For a long time Luci did not ask any questions.
She sat thinking about machines.

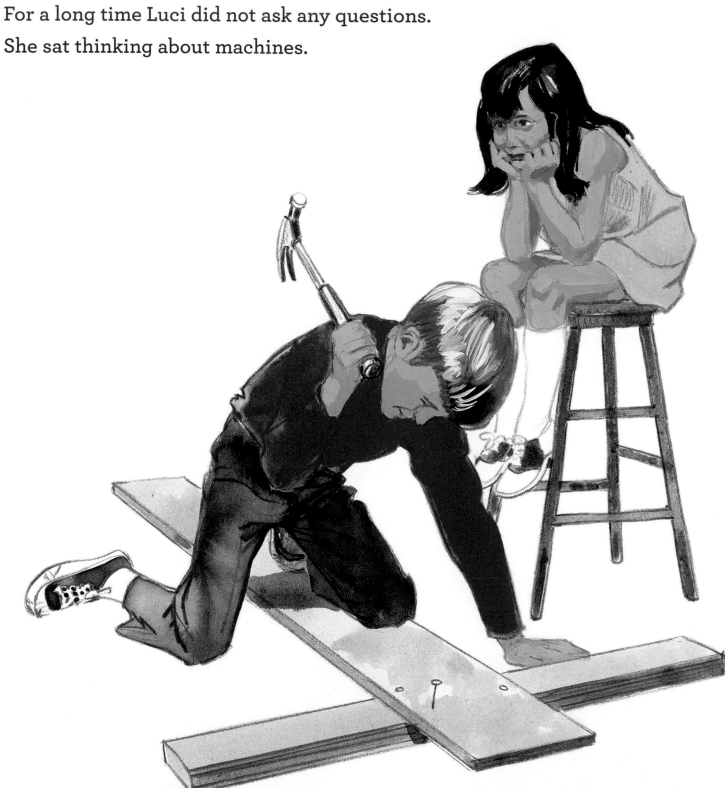

Michael hammered and nailed the wooden pieces together.
He was beginning to turn the first screw into the steering wheel
when Luci jumped up and asked, "How does a screwdriver work?
Is the screwdriver a machine, too?"

Luci was surprised when Michael said that a screwdriver is really
two machines. "It's a lever when you use it to pry something open,
but it's a wheel and axle when you use it to turn screws into wood."

"A wheel and axle? What is a wheel and axle?" asked Luci.

"A wheel and axle is like the steering wheel of our racing car. You turn a larger wheel here and a smaller wheel turns somewhere else. It makes your work easier to do, so it is called a machine. Do you see how a screwdriver looks and works like a steering wheel?"

A big smile stretched across Luci's face. Michael was a good teacher. She did understand what he showed her.

She took the screwdriver and put in one of the screws in the racing car. Then she put in several more.

"Now I know it's a machine. It made putting the screw in easier," Luci said, sitting down and again watching Michael closely.

All day long, with Luci's help, Michael worked on the racing car: first, the frame and then the steering wheel; later, the seat and wheels. The two of them used many different machines. They used levers, wheels and axles, wedges, hills, and screws. The two of them worked very well together. Michael thought that Luci learned quickly and was a good worker.

Luci watched Michael screwing a pulley on each side of the racing car frame. Before she could ask about the pulleys, Michael volunteered the information. "A pulley is a machine, too, you know. It can make lifting or turning things easier. These pulleys will turn the front wheels when a driver wants to turn the racing car. This is the last thing we have to do before trying it out."

Michael skillfully placed the pulleys along the frame.
He carefully threaded the steering ropes through the pulleys
and around the pulley wheels. Sure enough, they worked.

Luci turned the steering wheel, which, she thought to herself,
was a machine. "The front wheels turn," she said. Then she
added, "Maybe someday I'll be a mechanic or engineer.
Learning about simple machines and how they
can be used has been fun."

"I think you would be a great mechanic or engineer," praised Michael.

"When I started making this racing car, I did not know I would have a partner in putting it together. This is now *our* racing car. I'd like you to take the first ride with me."

Parent/Teacher Handbook

Introduction

The building of a racing car by Michael and his friend Luci is the framework for explanations about machines.

Inquiry Processes

Together, Michael and Luci illustrate several scientific processes. First, the process of application of knowledge to a problem is well illustrated. Michael's building of the racer demonstrates the use of simple machines in a realistic, practical manner. The process of inquiry is found in Luci's interest in learning about the tools Michael uses. Her questioning of him with "what" and "how" questions are inquiries that lead to understandings.

Content

A few years ago, some science texts listed six simple machines while others maintained there are four. The lever, the wheel and axle, the inclined plane, and the pulley are the basic simple machines. The wedge and the screw are variations of the inclined plane. The wedge is a double inclined plane. The screw is an inclined plane wrapped around a cylinder.

Currently, simple machines are not included in the *Next Generation Science Standards* because the subject is not considered a major science principle. Simple machines, however, are applications of science principles, so they can be used as an opportunity to investigate science principles.

Each simple machine is a device that enables a person to make work more convenient. Complex machines are combinations of the six simple machines. All machines, simple or complex, can be thought of as energy convertors. Energy in one form is used by the machine to produce energy in another form. For example, the lever may use muscular energy to produce mechanical energy.

A machine can help do work in three general ways: (1) by reducing the force needed to accomplish a task, (2) by changing the direction of the applied force, or (3) by increasing the speed with which work is done.

The following activities engage learners in investigations that reveal the physical science principles for which some simple machines were designed.

Science Activities

Observing the Advantage of an Inclined Plane

Obtain a wood or metal ruler, two large metal washers, three or four heavy books, and a spring scale—a scale that shows the force when you pull on it.

For test 1, hang the washers from the scale and lift it from the table to the top of the pile of books. Record the reading on the scale and use the ruler to measure the distance you raised the washers.

For test 2, place the ruler against the books to make a ramp. Use the scale to pull the washer from the table up the ramp to the top of the books. Record the reading on the scale and measure the distance you moved the washers.

Compare test 2 numbers with the test 1 numbers you recorded earlier. The work you did to lift the weight in each test is equal to the force you applied (the measure on the spring scale) multiplied by the distance you moved the object. If you did your measures carefully, the result of the math should be the same for both tests. But notice what is different in the measures. The inclined plane did not do the work for you, but it made the task easier. Pulling the weight a longer distance took less effort than pulling the weight straight up. You did the same total amount of work on the washer no matter how you got it from the table to the top of the books, but the small force used over a greater distance made the work easier.

If you had to move something very heavy to a higher level, would you lift it straight up or use a ramp? How do your numbers tell you which way is the "easier" way to lift something?

Finding Examples of Inclined Planes

Locate some examples of inclined planes around your home, in school, or in pictures from magazines. Here are some ideas to get you started: sloping floors in theaters or auditoriums, roads up hills, and ramps.

Find two or more objects that were probably moved up an inclined plane to get them inside a building.

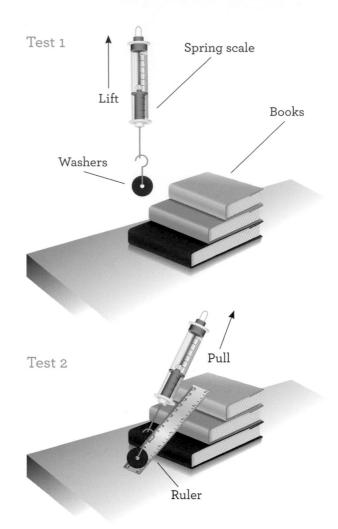

Additional activities can be found at www.nsta.org/machine.